THE SWEET FRUITS

Life Changing Steps And Inspiring True Stories.

PRISCILLA PEARL

RAJENDRAN

Title: The Sweetest Fruits
Language: English
Character set encoding: UTF-8

First published by

An Imprint of BlueRose Publishers

Head Office: B-6, 2nd Floor,
ABL Workspaces, Block B, Sector 4,
Noida, Uttar Pradesh 201301
M: +91-8882 898 898

DEDICATION

Firstly, I thank God for giving me this life, knowledge, wisdom, ability. When I look back to my journey it was just God's grace carrying this worthless woman forward.

This book is dedicated with greatest love to my parents and friends for their support and encouragement and constant love whose strength has made this journey the adventure of my life.

ACKNOWLEDGEMENTS

I was blessed to have the support of some people whom I want to express my sincere thanks:

To my parents for their constant love and support without your encouragement my gifts would have remained buried. I could not have done this without you. Your encouragement and love helped me to continue this journey.

Deep thanks to Matthew Rajesh for your encouragement.

Thanks to my friends who encouraged and prayed for me with loving heart.

Many thanks to all who contributed from publisher side.

Love you all.

FOREWORD

*I have had a great privilege to be a friend of Pearl,
and we have often talked about the sweetest fruit.
The topic is so interesting that I have encouraged
Pearl to write this book. Pearl's book combines what
qualities for life for better living which will help you
to boost up your confidence. I hope you can learn
something in these pages about the sweetest fruit in
one's life. I am deeply inspired by how we can shape
up our thoughts, life changing steps, real life story. If
you keep your attitude up if you make it as Pearl says
then you will see how much your life open right up
and blooms. All things being the same, person with
good qualities and good attitude will always go
further. Things won't be same all the time humans
are also like that only all are imperfect we should
forgive one another's   mistake with the kind heart
never think about the past and never criticize or
judge others let us hold and examine ourselves
projecting those criticism rather encourage one
another to experience more of joy each day and
make a better place for each other. Your life will be
more enjoyable when you have positive attitude. Your
outlook on life will be much better that the person
you live with all the time. There will be satisfaction
when you do small things with great love. You will
experience inner peace, love, joy like ever before. So,
as you hold this book in your hands, you are
beginning a journey that will shape up your thoughts
and has potential to improve yourself and relationship
with others. Isn't that beautiful? Just reading this
book will not change you it will help you to change
and you have to apply the qualities which you need.
Apply the truth, begin to power your mind, renew
the qualities within you, be with a positive attitude to
the people around you then your life will change for
a better. Forgiveness is a choice. Every day we arise
we have a choice on how we will view positively or*

negatively and how we interact with the people
around you. If you are filled with positivity and love
our interaction will fill others with joy and peace.
Pearl has done you a wonderful service by writing
the sweetest fruit. Apply love and positivity, and enjoy
the journey.

Matthew Rajesh

February 2023

PREFACE

Be the person who bears the sweetest fruits in life.

I know that a positive attitude is one's most priceless possession and one of your most valuable assets, it determines the overall quality of your life. Your attitude should be beautiful and powerful. Each of us has the power to develop a positive attitude that works for us, that improves the quality of our lives. Change your attitude, develop some qualities in your life. Win the bad with good. Apply some steps which can take to successfully walk out to genuine forgiveness. Stand strong in what you have done. Do not back to resentment. If you meet some people just take the good in them and ignore the bad. If someone have some good qualities just try to observe and learn them. Love one another as yourselves but that is not easy and not impossible also right slowly develop your attitude. Whenever we are tempted to criticize others lets us hold and examine ourselves. We have many gifts inside us if we are able to reap the sweetest fruits in our lives God will be pleased in that. You should not be scrupulous in the observance of the rules and rituals but become stupendous in practicing love, mercy, compassion and justice. Try to be more human in your dealings. Take steps to fill your heart with love, peace, joy that will help you to forgive freely and let go of bitterness. Reduce your worries learn to ignore negativity. As you step to enrich your life, allow the essential qualities, positivity and love to be your blue print. By applying the principles will provide you with enhanced instructionfor improving the overall quality of your life and help you reap sweetest fruits in your life that would make a better place for each other.

I wish you a wonderful journey to reap more sweetest fruits on your way.

Priscilla Pearl Rajendran.

INTRODUCTION

Each of us have the power to choose positive attitude over a negative one. If you want the attitude and qualities that works for you, that improves the quality of your life and your whole personality and enable you to accomplish your dreams, shape up your thoughts, renew your self-confidence, achieve your potential. In this book I will provide you some essential qualities for happy life, inspiring true stories that will help you to boost up yourself and to challenge the challenges of your life.

Here is the brief description of each of the chapters and some inspiring stories, real-life stories of people around me and some people I met and I hope that will boost yourself and will be a motivating one.

Chapter 1: Forgiveness – Form of love

Forgiveness is one of the most beautiful-word.

What makes this word such beautiful?

To forgive someone is not easy, but if you have the sweetest fruit called love you can forgive anyone. Forgiveness is the highest form of love. Once you learn to forgive you will receive peace and happiness. In this chapter I will offer you some keys to forgive and how blessed it is.

Chapter 2: Qualities for life

To be a better person and to make this place better to each other we need some sweetest fruits for life in this chapter I will give some themes which will help you to make an incredible difference in your lives and in the lives of people around you.

Chapter 3: Some people I met

In our day today life we meet lots of people. In this chapter I am going to share about some people I met in my life and what I learned from them with a touch of imagination.

Chapter 4: Hard work- The Sweetest fruit

To achieve our goal, we have to run with our dreams
make it true. On our pathway we have obstacles, failures,
challenges. Sometime we feel demotivated to complete our
journey. On this chapter I will tell you about one person
that will boost up in your journey. It is a real- life true
story.

Chapter 5: Purity of heart and mind

We are so much concerned about the exterior cleanliness
but fail to care for our mind and heart. In this chapter I will
share with you the tips to be with pure intension.

Chapter 6: Love

Love is one of the sweetest fruit and greatest gift we all
have. Love is kind and suffers long. Love fulfills the law.
When you are filled with love it automatically makes you
kind and makes you a wonderful person who does not
think wrong. In this chapter I will share how true love can
flow.

Chapter 7: Good for Bad

If anyone does bad for us, we feel very low and we get angry right....

But it is possible to win the bad with our good things. In
this chapter I will share a short message of good for bad.

Chapter 8: Develop your attitude

Your attitude is powerful tool for positive action. To trans-
form your attitude into action you must accept responsibili-

ty. In this chapter I will offer you the keys to controlling how you respond.

Chapter 9: Control your tongue

Our tongues are so powerful that they can ignite a wildfire of pain and trouble. In this chapter I will share some tips to control our tongue, temper, temptations and to practice meditation.

Chapter 10: Stay humble

Be conscious not to walk in pride or think yourself more highly than others. In this chapter I will share the blessings attached to staying humble.

Chapter 11: Do not judge

Judgement should be used in measure or it will measure you back

Chapter 12: Be busy doing good

You should not grow weary and do not loose heart while doing good for in due seasons you will reap its sweetest fruit.

Chapter 13: Be a winner

What is takes to become a winner

This is an investment to bear and reap good and sweetest fruit in your life.Your bitter fruit today will turn into sweetest fruit tomorrow

XVIII

Contents

PART PAGE

"Once you forgive a person do not criticize them by reminding their past mistake or bad time.

"Do not remind anyone about their past – let their inner wounds of heart heal."

FORGIVENESS - FORM OF LOVE

We all are not perfect everyone does a mistake in our lives. Everyone needs forgiveness. To forgive a person is not an easy task mentally we struggle a lot to forgive a person because that person might have cheated did wrong or might have spread rumors about you or hurt you with their words anything it might be. If a person feels sorry for what they did to you then they are eager to receive but it's hard for you to give. When your heart is filled with love you can forgive any person it is the highest form of love. Forgiveness is not an emotion that's why it is hard to give but when you decide to forgive a person it is a decision. You cannot work upon emotion but you can make the decision. There are some steps you have to take the right decision. You have to decide, once you have decided declare, stay strong, recognize your need to forgive. Declare if necessary. Stand strong in what you have done. Do not back to resentment because people around you will remind all wrong, they did to you, when you decided to forgive sometimes people around you will not let you to forgive some do it to spoil the relationship and some for their selfishness. The above steps themselves may be simple but putting them into practice may not be that simple. Once you are done with you will actually feel the inner peace. Be kind and compassionate to one another by forgiving each other. When you forgive a person that person you are giving them a chance to change themselves a better person.

There was a simple woman, she got married to a rich man, her brother I laws were very cunning that her husband did not knew. He thought his brothers are loving and caring. As her husband was elder son of their family so all asset was registered in his name. Few years passed couple was blessed with a baby boy. When that baby boy was just three months old the husband of that woman was murdered by her brother in laws. They mixed a poison in his dinner and her husband passed away that night itself. How painful it will be for her. After the funeral of her husband her brother in laws threatened her saying if you will stay in our house, we will kill your baby. They might have thought she will own the assets. She moved out from there and went to her hometown. With lots of struggle she raised up her child, educated him and after some ages she shared about the above past story of her. The child got angry he told I will take revenge of them who killed my father. Do you know what she replied to her child just forgive them my dear child best revenge is to prove yourself. Be well educated raise your standard. Just do this and never ask anything about this to anyone. That boy also forgave them and developed his career and earned more assets than they got cheated.

MY QUOTES ON FORGIVENESS:

"Once you forgive a person do not criticize them by reminding their past mistake or bad time."

"Do not remind anyone about their past – let their inner wounds of heart heal."

QUALITIES FOR LIFE

The essence of mankind is the human quality. The purpose of our life needs to be positive and we must develop basic human qualities –self-control, kindness, goodness, faithfulness, gentleness, peace, love,patience and to be wise.

SELF-CONTROL

Helping yourself can increasingly conquer your temptations and learn to embrace the fruit of self-control. It helps you to keep your mind focused to avoid the temptations of your desires. Many worldly temptations can be strong, but your self-control should be stronger than that. Develop the ability to demonstrate your own self-control.

You should develop the ability to manage urges and impulses, ability to regulate emotional responses. Some find hard to manage strong emotions that leads to over-reaction or bad moods. It is a great deal of will power and personal control.

Some people do what the other person says just to satisfy the opposite person. If a person is diabetic with high blood sugar levels and he is under treatment to lower his blood sugar levels, one day his friend comes to meet him. His wife offers tea, snacks and sweets to his friend. His friend said to him you also take some sweets I will not eat alone. Without telling anything he ate that sweet thinking his friend will get disappointed. The next day he some complications in his health, he went for checkup and his blood sugar levels were hiked than before and his doctor recommended him to start with the insulin injection. Why such complications, he might I told his friend that do not mistake me I will not eat the sweet as I am undergoing treatment for high sugar levels or simply, he might have told I don't want now. He did not have, self-control to avoid that sweet.

Whether the matter is big or small we must have control in ourself to choose the good and avoid the bad that power is a fruit of self-control. In every area of your life, you should have self-control, do not do a thing because everyone are doing, you should have the control to choose your own way. Self-control is also important for maintaining healthy behaviors. Reap the fruit of self-control to develop the ability of your emotions, thoughts and behavior in the face of temptations and impulses. Always avoid situations where you know you will confront temptations. Key to self-control is your own ability and understandings. Self control helps you to be self strice,self disciplined,restraint,to strengthen your mind,to be stable,emotion regulation and to control your emotions.

KINDNESS

Kindness begins with caring, being tender hearted and compassionate. Truly kind people will find opportunities to show kindness. Every person deserves to be treated with respect and kindness. I have some people being rude with the poor people or with their helpers, they are also a simple human being like us they also have heart, feelings like us. Being rude with poor people are pride for some people. Kindness is humbly giving of ourselves in love and mercy to others who may not be able to give anything in return. Kindness means a way of thinking that leads to doing thoughtful deeds for others.

Sometimes if your friends or relatives are going through rough times your kind words should be their strong mental support it will boost them, you can at-least make things a little more pleasant. Even the simplest act of heartfelt kindness may be the one act that begins to soften someone's hurting heart.

There were two women one woman was rich and educated and another woman was from a middleclass family, both were standing near a railway station. A poor beggar man was asking for food no one gave he came near that rich woman and ask please give me some food she shouted at him another woman saw that and came near them and asked the beggar what happened he told give me some food then she went to the nearby restaurant and brought food parcel and gave him. Such kind she was.

Kindness is the sweetest fruit that will stimulate you to loving actions and to be kind to one another.

GOODNESS

Goodness can be seen in our actions but our heart also has to be pure. The goodness of yours should be demonstrated in your lives every day. You should be filled with goodness inside, outside you should have a heart that seeks goodness. The goodness as a sweetest fruit is not merely behavior, but an excellence of character. Grow the fruit of goodness so that you can live a fulfilling life full of righteous love.

There was a poor woman living in a small village, she had four children. One day she was on the way to her home from her work place. On the way there was a banyan tree and under the tree there was a new born girl baby. The poor woman looked here and there and asked whose baby is this the people around there told we do not know since afternoon baby is lying here, we do not know who kept there. The woman took that baby to her home raised up with her four children like her own child. She educated her, and did everything like how she did for her children she did not do any partialities. What a heart of goodness she had.

Goodness is a fruit that binds and brings hope in the midst of despair.

FAITHFULNESS

Faithfulness is a foundational character that is necessary for good life. There may be many times we may not feel the faithfulness but we may choose to trust. We should learn to be to be faithful and it requires trust and loyalty. Our faithfulness allows us to trust. You should be loyal and true.

There was a business man, suddenly he had financial loss in his business. He was in a need of money. One day he going to a bank to ask loan, on the way he saw a bag he took the bag and opened it to see whether he gets their contact number. A purse full of money was there and no one was around him. Immediately he took the bag and handed to police station. They informed the owner they came and gave compensation to this business man, but he did not receive the compensation and said it was my responsibility I did not expect anything from you.

Whatever the situation it would be you have to be loyal and true to your family, at your work place and everyone. The quality of faithfulness is the gracious fruit in your life.

GENTLENESS

A gentle person is mild-mannered towards people, moderate, considerate, thoughtful to others, yielding and friendly. A person who is gentle does not resort to using force to get things done.

But very often people are told that this soft approach to people is not suitable for survival in our world. Your gentleness should be known to everyone. It takes a great strength of character and self-control to be gentle in many situations. When you treat others gentle you gain trust and respect. Being gentle makes others more willing to listen you. Fighting destroys relationship and take so much time to repair. You can prevent inciting anger by choosing to respond with gentleness. Doing so creates a closer connection and as an added bonus you will save your time and hardships.

Your fruit of gentleness should be evident to all.

PEACE

Peace is the strongest human desire whether it be peace between other people or peace within our own minds. Without the fruit called peace we cannot have the fruit of kindness.

During pandemic some of you might have experienced anxiety. People were stressed about finances, family, children, work, sickness etc. In such circumstances it is difficult to find peace.

Peace is a gift for all it is amazing and hard to understand. Guard your heart and mind. The situation might be opposite with lots of obstacles and circumstances but be peaceful. It is tough but not impossible, the fruit will not ripen in our lives overnight, as we mature everything will change totally and with that our fruit will grow within us. We all simple human being everything will take its own time for success.

Some people will have everything, life will be smoothly going but they lose their inner peace because of greed for more money, jewels, wealth etc. Money is important for our lives but we cannot buy everything by money. Sometimes people around you might criticize you, try to break you emotionally but those words should not affect you. Stay strong always, strengthen up your emotions, with small eyes you can see great things.

Cultivate the fruit called peace to strong, happy and peaceful always

INNER PEACE IS ALWAYS BEAUTIFUL.

LOVE

Love is totally different from our today's culture. In our day today life you meet different kinds of people some people talk sweetly to you but behind your back they dig pits, one should not be like that. Love is self-sacrifice, putting others' needs before your own. There are many people who lost their families there are so many children who lost their parents they just love, try to spend some time with such kind of beautiful souls you will definitely a great happiness. These kinds of people just want someone to spend little time to share the things going on their mind. In old age homes there are many people forsaken by their children they might have lived a luxurious life, but when their children leave here and go how their mind will be, just take a minute to think of that. When you get time try to give some time with such people.

Love your enemies it is really a tough job but not impossible let your reaction change their actions. Love is not rude or jealous.

Give the fruit of love generously you will definitely receive the fruit of love graciously.

PATIENCE

Patience leads to a happy life. Patience is quite hope and trust that things will turn out right. You are tolerant and accepting of difficulties and mistakes. Patience is a commitment to the future. It helps to accomplish our goals, no matter what obstacles comes. Patience helps one feel satisfied in life, helps achieve inner peace. In my personal life I was short tempered in nature since childhood, but when I started to cultivate patience in my life I was satisfied and learnt how to ignore negativity, negative people and how not to react for their negative sayings or unnecessary arguments. It ultimately helped me to make better decisions and to be a better person.

Be patient, achieve more.

BE WISE

Wisdom is quality of having experiences, knowledge, and good judgement. Much wisdom is learned one time. Growing in knowledge makes you wise. Becoming wise means to grow in our thought change. Changes in life comes when heart change and thought change coincide. When one's heart and thoughts are change, life change should be the end result. You will have a foundation that will never change. Necessary changes become the source of nourishment and growth.

Sow the seed of change in your heart, thought, and life, reap the fruit of being wise.

SOME PEOPLE I MET

AN OLD WOMAN

Once I went to Chennai, there I met an old woman, she had four children, her husband passed away few years back. She was from a rich family. Her children were well educated all of them got settled abroad, but no one was looking after her. No one talks with her and she was unaware that their children sold all the assets here. She was left alone and one the neighbor helped her who was once a maidservant at her home. Then she started a small business at home. Then she rented a house shifted there and now she is earing well in her business which is enough for her living. I asked her if you want any help you can ask us, she replied your love is enough for me. People here are relatives and children for me.

When you are a child your parents take care of you, fulfill your needs, educate you give you everything you ask. Then it is your responsibility to take care of your parents in their old age.

Do not forsake your parents who made you the person whom you are today.

AN YOUNG MAN

Once I met a person it was an official meet,we became good friends.One day he told about his family,since childhood whatall he came across,he was born in a poor family,his dad was a drunkard due to which his family suffered a lot.Daily his father use to drink alcohol and use to abuse his mother,this was going on regularly, when he was in his tenth standard one night the same happened and next was his tenth board exam,he got angry and asked his dad if you fight like this daily how can we all study.Immediately his dad fired all his books and the next day was his exam he went to his friend's house but no one was ready to give book for him.He just revised in mind whatever he studied till that day and next day he wrote the exam.He told his situation to his class teacher and she arranged the books for him.His dad won't let him study, in that situation he use to study the whole night after his dad wents to sleep.After some days the results were out and he passed out as a school topper.Ater his schooling he worked in tea shops,hotels,in paddy fields to continue his education.With lots of challenges he complted his Ph.D and now he is working in a reputed company and making good money.

Challenges are meant to be challenged,work harder to achieve your goal,once you achieve it work more harder to achieve many more.

HARDWORK - THE SWEETEST FRUIT

A boy was born a middleclass agricultural family. His father worked at Central Railway(Mumbai) and mother looked after the agriculture in their home town. He was the elder son in his family. He was very hardworking since childhood and obedient child to his parents. He grew during his teens he went to Mumbai with his father. He worked hard, and tried applying for job in railways after some days he got his appointment to join Indian Railways after joining he was loyal to his work did much hard work and purchased many acres of agricultural land, looked after his siblings, and did everything what all his mother said whatever she asked he purchased for his mom, dad and siblings too. Did his sisters marriages looked after his sister's families. Through his hard work he got promoted as an electrical engineer at Indian Railways. He got married and even after marriage he listened what his mother said. Whatever property he purchased was registered by his mother's name. When his brothers got married his mother gave all the asset to his younger brother and cheated him. He built a house that also his mother gave to his brother. His mother and siblings totally cheated him. He moved on and started working harder and harder and earned more than what he lost or being cheated and proved himself. The success what he achieved was only from his consistent hard work.

The person about whom you read this much time is my father.

My father always tells me do not believe anyone not even me and your mom, just believe God and be consistent is your work whatever you do.

Hard work is also essential fruit of life. When we work hard consistently and with perseverance. Only hard work helps you to overcome the fear of failure. Hard work is always a base line for success.

You might have failed somewhere in life do not stop yourself there itself, challenges are meant to be challenged. Do not be afraid, trust yourself, trust your talents, hard work gives you something when you persistently fight for it.

Do develop the quality of perseverance and consistent hard work and reap the sweetest fruit called success and shine brightly.

PURITY OF HEART AND MIND

When you have a quality of obedience, you humble yourself and walk in the strength to pursue purity of heart and mind. You are not strong enough or wise or godly enough to pursue purity on our own. It needs pure living that follows purity of heart. Self-control helps you progress toward purity; you must guard your heart to cultivate virtue. By orienting your life toward purity, you should no longer feel impure desires. Set limits on your behavior and have an escape plan to avoid indulging in what you know is wrong. Strive towards what is good. Measure yourself. The essential is that of being pure in heart and mind.

You are so concerned about the exterior cleanliness but fail to care your mind and heart. You should not be negative minded, greedy, wicked, jealous, hatred, bad intended theses all actually makes a person unclean making yourself and others miserable. Some people create problems in others life, they peep into others life, they will spread rumors about someone, some people talk like honey with you and talk evil behind your back. Some people are full of negative vibes but act positively.

Be concerned about conducting your interior life, love humanity with purity of heart and mind and love. Develop the discipline that will lead you to pure heart.

The feeling of the heart is both positive and negative. Some emotions spur people together in brotherly love and compassion. Some root individuals in stubbornness, disdain and pride. One such emotion is jealousy a form of covetousness. It changes the way you should perceive others or yourselves. At the root of covetousness, jealousy and envy is pride. You need to put covetousness, jealousy and envy. Start to set free from the bondage of jealously.

Bear more good fruits for life.

Have a pure heart, pure mind, pure soul, pure intension.

Beauty lies in it.

LOVE

LOVE FULFILLS LAW

Today some of you hold on to the rules and rituals while compromising humanity in bargain. You should not take delight in your observance of rules and regulations but in the promotion of love, mercy, compassion and justice. Do not use liberty as an opportunity but through love serve one another. Love all as yourselves. Be more human in your dealings.

LOVE ENSIGNS OUR LIVING

True love can only flow from a heart that is full of love. When your heart is filled in greater measure it flows from you to others. A love that embraces everyone rich and poor, high and low equally without any distinction. Love your enemies, revenge is not the remedy. Love all hate none. Take courage, be convinced that forgiving is strength. Make the channel of love. Always be happy, live positive.

LITTLE THINGS WITH GREAT LOVE

Love transforms things. When a small act is performed with love it becomes huge.

Huge to the person sharing the love, huge to the person receiving. Huge to anyone who happens to witness the exchange. Saint Teresa of Calcutta spent her life pouring it out for other people every day in the simplest ways. You cannot win hearts and minds with violence and oppression but you can win it with love.

One day me and my parents went to a supermarket there one old man was working in vegetable packing section we were looking for some other groceries there. At that time, he came and told excuse me, please do not mistake me at our place there is one orphanage facing financial issues there are fifty children there can you please do something for that children or can you give food or groceries for the children. He joined his hands and asked for that children.

One day my friend, called me and asked a help for a student. She was studying final year of bachelor's degree and collages fees was pending. We don't need big thing just do, little things with love to make a better place for each other

RELATIONSHIP IS THE ESSENCE OF LOVE

We are created to be in relationship with people. Some struggle because of past pain in relationships. It takes dedication, love and forgiveness. You are called to exercise the essence of love in your relationship that is love, compassion, kindness, gentleness, mercy with your fellow beings, in your families and society. Human being cannot exist without relationships. You

have to live in identity of love in all your relationships. Love everyone with the genuine love
for each other.

Be the sweetest fruit in your life bearing the
essential nutrient called love

GOOD FOR BAD

If you are hurt by harsh words or unkind actions from another person.it is ok to acknowledge those feelings. You should not ignore the pain you feel, but you do not have let that pain fuel negative response. You simply have to walk away from mean people which takes a great amount of strength, dignity, and courage. Commend yourself in every way in great endurance, in troubles, hardships and distress in purity, understanding, patience and kindness. Allow yourself to feel the pain. Refuse to seek revenge and try to be kind. Be kind to the mean people and show the love through your humble actions.

Go forth and do wonders.

DEVELOP YOUR ATTITUDE

BEAUTIFUL ATTITUDE

Having a positive attitude are good and easy to see more enjoyment of each day and stronger relationships. Developing yourself keep you part to play in keeping your attitude right. Use the opportunities to bless others through your beautiful good attitude. Choose the steps that leads to good attitude.

POWERFUL ATTITUDE

A positive attitude causes a chain reaction of positive thoughts and outcomes. A positive attitude is a powerful force. Your attitude is a commitment to generate positive results in your lives. Allow the power to change you through renewal of your minds. To develop an attitude that helps you live life to its fullest, your attitude is nothing but an outward reflection of what resides on the inside. To change your attitude into powerful attitude you must change your heart first.

GRATITUDE IS AN ATTITUDE

It is faith that keeps our life the routine works of everyday and seldom, you may think about those people who make the day a comfortable one for you. From rising till retiring many people contribute to the smooth functioning of our life. Take some time to just recollect, those insignificant person behind your best day and thank them with your simple gesture of thankfulness.

ATTITUDE OF REPENTANCE

Repentance is a change of heart that leads to change in the direction of life. If you did a mistake, it is ok no one is perfect here. People around you may criticize you for your mistake, bear the criticize then only you can achieve success. Once you repent do not change your attitude for anyone or anything. Renew yourself do not repeat the mistake. Develop a clean heart and steadfast spirit within you.

Repentance is not just a part of transformation but is an attitude of heart with accompanying actions. Try to pursue righteousness and fight the good fight. A change of heart should always translate into behaviors that are visible to others.

POSITIVE ATTITUDE

Positive and negative thoughts both are powerful but have opposite results. The gratifying soul is about spreading positive vibes and being the best version of yourself. Positive thinking improves our life. Create a positive environment to live in because the people you spend your time with the information you let influence your mind will have a huge effect on your attitude and how you think about things. Be grateful for what you have. Focus on solutions to any problems.

Reduce your worries, do not let negative people or their words ruin your thinking. Stayaway from negative people, surround yourself with good people.

Do not give up, keep going.

CONTROL YOUR TONGUE

Our tongues can ignite a wildfire of pain and trouble. In-fact there is some research that indicates the words actually change the physical makeup of our brain, genetic materials. Develop the quality to control your tongue, temper, temptation. A positive word might increase our cognitive function while a negative word might district it. Words can hurt, use them with caution. Some people always talk to remind our past, gossip about others, spread rumors. Your words should not hurt or disturb someone's peace of mind.

Avoid gossips and do not take your tongue for granted. Make use of it to motivate others, to bring positive impact in someone's life, to teach good things, to comfort others, and to make others smile.

Use it wisely.

STAY HUMBLE

Be conscious not to walk in pride or think yourself more highly than others because pride is of flesh and if not stopped, can lead to other forms of sin. In your interaction or dealings with others be the one willing to help others. Let your humility be so true and pure, it is so contagious that those around you desire to emulate you. Pride will draw and repel people away from you, leading to closed doors but humility will open the heart of people towards you and keep the doors of opportunities opened constantly to you. Make up your mind daily intentionally stay humble, no matter the level of success in your life.

STAY HUMBLE AND KIND

Learn to resist the proud, be kind to one another, be tenderhearted. Forgive one another. Humble people care for the poor and oppressed. They feel their responsibility in helping them. These two values coexist. Humanity springs forth from our trust. The care, concern and responsibility towards the underprivileged can cause to reap a fruit called happiness.

Open your mouth for speechless, judge righteously. It involves being just and doing justice. Show mercy as mercy is the fruit of compassion. Mercy is the compassionate treatment of those in need. Life is a gift so walk humbly, help the people living in poverty. Humility is perhaps one of the hardest-thing for us to show we require to be centered, focused and to keep our heart balanced on love.

DO NOT JUDGE

We cannot expect good from evil minded person and any evil from good hearted people. A person's speech discloses the cultivation of one's mind. The words that come from the mouth could be a blessing, curse, praise, anger, hurting, loving, healing, comforting and soothing depending on the deposition of mind and heart nurtured by the person. You can examine yourselves whether you are a good tree or a bad tree from the way we speak and the way we accomplish our deeds. Train your mind and guard your thoughts, watch over your mouth and excel in your words and deeds. You should not declare someone's disgrace to others, you should not speak evil of one another. You should constantly be examining your own heart and your own actions. When you focus on correcting your own, you will have an attitude of humility. Do not pass judgements on others. Do not judge others motive. Do not gossip. Judge yourselves

Always be a good tree yielding good fruit.

BE BUSY DOING GOOD

Do not grow weary while doing good, for in due season you will reap the fruit of doing good if you do not loose your heart. We live in a modern world that has lot of evil in it. There is lot of hate. There is lot of selfishness. You are still supposed to have the fruit of goodness inside you. The only way people are going to know you is by your actions. Your good behavior has the ability to reveal your love to those around you. Let your light shine before others so that they may see your good work. You should not wait for time, season, reason for accomplishing any good work. Sometimes you may often hesitate to do good on certain days and times. Sometimes you fail to do and refuse to do even those activities that charity demands for us. Go beyond all these and be concerned about not missing any opportunity that awaits us to do good.

Do good deeds and be blessed with the sweetest fruit called blessings.

BE A WINNER

We all are born to be a winner or loser. There is a process to win. Winners have different mindset, specific behavior and habits. To be a winner, you need to develop and change some habits that will allow you to win. There are certain things that set winners apart from everyone else, so that you can become winner in the game of life.

You need to set your goals, create habit that supports your goal, do not waste time, have a productive day, accept responsibility in every area of your life, embrace failure, use your time wisely, plan your day, perseverance is the most important key, be consistent in your work, cultivate patience, work hard and smart as well. Be brave and bold and do not worry. In life you face hard times, it is not always to take everything at best.

Try again and again, be the best. There will be obstacles and problems in life face them. Keep all your worries and hard times apart and keep going. Be committed.

Index

About the Author

Priscilla Pearl Rajendran is from Mumbai. She is pursuing her PhD and a working professional. She is a writer by passion. She is moving in her life keeping the purpose of bringing positive impact and change in society through her writings. Her favorite things in life are reading, nature, photography, blogging, digital content creating, writing, gardening, drawing and painting. She believes in the motto *"A positive mind finds opportunity in everything."* Through her book, she wants to convey the same message.